I AM MY OWN ORANGE COUNTY

I0098888

selected writings 1990 to 1997
by Rick Lupert

11th Anniversary
Edition~2008

I AM MY OWN ORANGE COUNTY (11th Anniversary Edition)

Layout and Design ~ Rick Lupert
Section Title Page Concept ~ Amit Shamis
About the Author Photo ~ Addie Lupert
Back Cover Photo ~ Robert Wynne
Illustrations page 69 and 81 ~ Arash Saedinia

"I'm The Writer" originally appeared in Poetry Ink # 11 ~ "The Journey Of The Sperm" originally appeared in 51% Vol.2, #1 ~ "Unexpected Lips" originally appeared in Blue Satellite Vol.2, # 1 ~ "You (are art incarnate)" originally appeared in You'll Wonder How You Ever Got Along Without It Vol.1, # 1 ~ "Apartment" originally appeared in *Beyond The Valley of the Contemporary Poets* ~ "Five Dollar Sunglasses and Venice Pizza" originally appeared as "Venice Pizza" in Blue Satellite Vol. 1, # 1 ~ "Dirty Coffee" originally appeared in Poetry Ink # 12 ~ "Coffee Is Not a Drink For Pussies" originally appeared in Blue Satellite Vol. 2, # 2 ~ "Blender" and "The Lone Mosher" originally appeared in Caffeine issue 10 ~ "Ants" originally appeared in Caffeine issue 5 ~ "No Fish Blues" originally appeared in Caffeine Issue 8 ~ "Untitled" originally appeared in Caffeine issue 12.

Thanks to Charles Ardinger for inspiring the title poem. Thanks to Arash Saedenia for saying "You should call the book 'I Am My Own Orange County'" and for the artwork. Thanks to Brendan Constantine, June Melby and the artist formerly known as Matthew Niblock for reading at the original publication party on May 10, 1997 at the Cobalt Cafe in Canoga Park, California. Thanks to Addie, who I love, for retyping this book and for tolerating that I wrote it.

818-904-1021
or
15522 Stagg St. # 12, Van Nuys, CA 91406
or
Rick@PoetrySuperHighway.com
or
PoetrySuperHighway.com

11th Anniversary Edition ~ First Printing ~ November 2008

CONTENTS

Geography

Food and Drink

Animals (mostly insects)

Stories

Giant Hoochie Dinosaurs That Lick Your Eyeballs

Re-Introduction

Welcome back to *I Am My Own Orange County*. For years I've been threatening to re-release this book. Mainly to win arguments and influence poodles.

Don't read this book. The word 'penis' appears 183% more times than in the original 1997 edition. This is far too many times. No one should have to read a book in which the word 'penis' appears twenty-two times. (Not counting the two in this paragraph.)

Over the years people have written to me, or spoken to me in person and said things like "When are you going to re-release this book." I usually responded with the tale of the great hard drive crash of 1999 and talked sheepishly about having to re-type the whole thing. People volunteered to retype it. They would volunteer out-loud and then they would pretend to be dead. One man held his breath for three days just to convince me rather than retype this book.

Are you still here? Please remove the children from the immediate area. Please remove the children from the surrounding communities. At this point, it would be better if you didn't have children.

Once on a van-ride between the General Mitchell International airport in Milwaukee and a lovely camp in Oconomowoc, Wisconsin I sat next to a boy. He asked me if I knew if Rick Lupert would be at the camp. I told him I was sure that he would be and that, in fact, I was Rick Lupert. He became excited. He stopped talking to me and started making cellular telephone calls to people who he knew to tell them he was on a van with Rick Lupert. Apparently the poems in this book had influenced him at a young age. I apologize for this.

If you do have children, or know of children, make sure to take them to the dentist. It is best to wait until they have teeth and also to not wait until their teeth are gone. The dentist will put his or her hands inside your child's mouth. If you have two children, they will have to take turns and you will not receive a discount. The dentist should not mention his or her penis. If he or she does, you should find another dentist.

It would have been great to release this special edition for its tenth anniversary. As it is I am just barely getting it out during the eleventh anniversary year. If I had waited much longer it would have been the twelfth anniversary. Of the numbers ten, eleven and twelve, ten is the best in terms of excitement. There is a small amount of excitement that eleven has two "ones" right next to each other; but it does not equal the excitement of ten. Ten is a milestone. Ten is a thing to look forward to and celebrate. Eleven is just okay. Twelve is the bastard child of thirteen and negative one.

I did the math. It really is 183% more. These figures would hold up in court. This figures would hold up on a piece of paper if they were written down and then held up by a hand. It would not need to be witnessed. You could just trust the person who said they held up the paper. It's not rocket science.

I Am My Own Orange County is my sophomore release. It is also my most sophomoric release. It tries to be funny and entertaining and occasionally surreal in that Richard Brautigan kind of way. This is all okay. I support you if you enjoy it and I understand if you are embarrassed for me by it.

God help us all.

November 22, 2008

Introduction

Someone recently described exposure to my work as a similar experience to getting kicked in the teeth. I wasn't exactly sure how to respond to this beyond recommending a good dentist. This, of course, was a sham as I have not been to the dentist in several years. The best I could do would be to front with 1-800-DENTIST and hope for the best. By the way, this book was not endorsed by 1-800-DENTIST but I do wish them the best.

What exactly does it mean to be one's own Orange County? I'll tell you. It's about being self critical. When you read your poetry in Orange County, you'll find the audience more interactive; often critiquing your poem out-loud while you read it. Now, read the title poem of the book and put the rest together.

It's not that I don't think dental hygiene is important. I brush and floss every day. My teeth are doing fine. I have no problem smiling with my mouth open. In fact, I am doing so right now.

This is my second book, and first true anthology of my work, collected over the last seven years, featuring many of the things I've had published various places, as well as things so special that I am the only one who agreed to publish them.

I'm not trying to portray myself as a member of the Osmond family. Now there were some teeth. Shiny, shiny shiny! I'm sad that the Osmonds don't get as much attention these days. This, of course, is also how I feel about Mr. T.

I cheated when I published my first book *Paris: It's The Cheese.* Although a fine body of work, it only contained poems I had written during a two week period in Paris. It wasn't representational of what I had written during the six years I had been writing.

When I was in Paris I saw a dubbed-to-French version of The A-Team. When Mr. T. spoke, instead of the angry, yet powerful voice I had been accustomed to, there was a white-guy French voice. It made me realize that Paris is not such an easy city to live in for someone like me.

One thing which I think made *Paris: It's The Cheese* good was it's thematic nature. I have tried to capture that in *I Am My Own Orange County* by arranging the book into ten themed sections. This approach also made it easier for me to pick poems from the overwhelming amount of material I have written. (It may well be that my next book is also a collection of writings from 1990 to 1997.)

Who am I kidding? My teeth are rotting out my face along with every one of my internal organs. I have rotting organ syndrome. It's caused by being pompous and never going to the dentist. My spleen is rotting most of all. Soon I will have a splenectomy.

The truth is, I write to entertain. Occasionally something with more depth surfaces amidst my attempts at humor. I don't take myself too seriously, and am at the same time, much too self critical. That's what this book is about. (and all of the individual poems are about their own individual things too.)

There used to be laws which prohibited one from reading poetry in public places if one didn't have a full compliment of bodily organs. This is why I fully compliment my organs before I read my work. You might hear me saying "You're such a good liver," or "I am in love with my trachea" before any given reading. If I had a uterus, there would be no end to my self internal-grandiosity.

Thanks to everyone who has supported me in every way in my writing adventures. I wouldn't be able to do it without you.

March 30, 1997

In a way, we are all our own Orange County...

meeting younger versions of older people

Christopher Reeve

A young Christopher Reeve
just came in and sat down in the coffee house
He eyed three high school girls
who came in a few minutes later
It's a good thing he wasn't the old Christopher Reeve
because then those girls would have been too young for him.

Cosmo Kramer

A young Cosmo Kramer
came into the coffee house
ordered a muffin.
Only his hair was much more in tune
with the world around him
than the real Cosmo Kramer.
The old Cosmo Kramer
has lived a long enough time to de-synchronize his hair.

Marc Chagall

A young Marc Chagall
just came in and hung his art up on the coffee house walls.
Only the colors were all wrong
and the framing jobs were mediocre.
The old Marc Chagall
sure knew how to frame a stained glass window.

David Schwimmer

A young David Schwimmer
just came into the coffee house,
ordered a mocha, sat down.
Only I don't watch that show so it meant nothing to me.
The old David Schwimmer
also means nothing to me.

Mikhail Baryshnikov

A young Mikhail Baryshnikov
just came into the coffee house with his mother
only he was only five years old
and hadn't developed any of the characteristics
of the old Mikhail Baryshnikov yet.
The old Mikhail Baryshnikov
has had a lifetime
to develop his Baryshnikovian characteristics.

Man With No Ass

A man with no ass came into the coffee house
and I felt bad for him
so I passed around a hat
and raised fifty three dollars
which I gave to him
so he could put a down-payment
on getting himself a new ass.

Rick Lupert

A young Rick Lupert
walked into the coffee house poetry book in hand
ordered some tea and sat down.
Only he was writing beautiful poems
which touched the souls of everyone who read them.
The old Rick Lupert
only writes poems to pick up chicks.

songs of myself

I'm The Writer

I'm the writer
I always have a pen
I play Scrabble just to keep in practice with all the words
I don't need to play Scrabble because I know all the words
People come up to me who I've never met before and say
"You're that writer guy"
My identity precedes me
Things I witness are not other people's experiences,
Rather they are material for my work
I use metaphors
My work screams to be interpreted
Sometimes it's so complicated,
I don't even understand what I've written
Some women worship the paper I write on
Some men worship the paper I write on
My mother worships the paper I write on
Both men and women ask to model nude for my poems
My work appears in many places
including, but not limited to
books, magazines, newspapers, bathroom walls,
the inside of matchbooks
and the internet
Soon it will be beamed into outer space
for the benefit of culturally literate aliens
and God
The dictionary is my Bible
I am constantly quoting from it
I make people laugh
I piss people off
I offer a full range of emotions
Sometimes I leave the house without underwear
I do this to increase my consciousness
It always works
I'm the most conscious person I know
I'm the writer
I write
That's what I do

Autobiography

For me,
life began at birth
I spent the first part of life
as a child,
The second
as a young person,
And currently exist
as a person
who people perceive as being very young,
Although I'm not as young as all that.

During my life,
I've done many things.
My future plans include
the doing of many other things,
Including,
but not limited to
Skydiving.

The cause of my death
will be a lack of oxygen to my brain.
This will be brought about by natural causes,
or something.

My death will occur at the end of my life.
It is because of this
that I am linked to all other people
who have lived,
Including the famous ones.

My death will be an example
of the missing link
between life and death.
It is for this,
that I will be remembered.

The Less I write

The less I write
The less I have to spend on journals to write in
The more money I have for food
The more I eat and get fat
The less experiences I have to write about
As I get bigger
The less I become.

I am A Sinner

I am a sinner
I've said the wrong things
to the wrong people
at the wrong times
and then I've murdered them all
and eaten their bodies.
I'm not aware of what any of the laws are
and therefore don't follow any of them.
I have lunch with Satan every Tuesday
Not only does he already own my soul,
but I owe him three others.
I have mixed every kind of drug,
with every kind of alcohol
and then driven the streets of Los Angeles under their influence
aiming my car directly at
newlywed couples,
infants,
and frail old people.
When this doesn't work,
I usually set myself on fire,
run into day care centers
and hug all the children.
I only date married women
or people under fifteen,
or women of any age
who will take it in the ass
all the while screaming
"Rock my hiney hard, Satan Boy."
All my clothing is made out of dead animal fur,
all my furniture is constructed out of rain-forest tree wood
(except for my entertainment center which is made out of ele-
phants tusks)
and the only foods I eat are
veal,
dolphin,

meat from endangered species,
and head cheese.
For creative output, I write poetry,
but only misogynistic verse
or poems about my penis.
I believe the world revolves around my penis.
and so does it.
These are my sins.
This is my confession.
Please,
forgive me.

I Take Risks

I take risks
Like the time I jumped off the Empire State Building
Fortunately they had just closed off the street
for a spontaneous mattress convention
that had broken out.
I take risks

sex, dating and other body parts

The Journey of the Sperm

The journey of the sperm is a treacherous one, indeed.
During ejaculation,
Millions of sperm are shot into the vaginal cavity,
much like reverse bungee jumping.
Many of these sperm are so excited
they die trying to fertilize
the first round object they encounter.
This parallels the behavior of some men.
Continuing on their journey,
many sperm choose the wrong fork on the fallopian tube road
ending up dead
in an eggless sperm graveyard.
This could be avoided,
if the sperm would stop and ask for directions.
This parallels the behavior of some men.
Of course there are no signs posted
pointing the sperm in the correct direction,
leaving them confused about the appropriate action to take.
This parallels the behavior of some women, and men,
and provides us special insights
as to the nature of human relationships.

Video Store

I continually return
to the foreign film section
searching for
the cultured erotic she.

Garden of Evedom

Men don't have it as easy as women
as exemplified in our one less rib situation
It's not easy trying to compete in a world
where half the population had a rib up on you
Please don't expect as much from us
Special parking would be appreciated

Mannequin I

Today
I fell in love with a mannequin in May Company
She was short
She was beautiful
Desperate times

Mannequin II

I passed by my mannequin love three times today
It might have been four
I said hello
I decided to call her Ruth

Mannequin III

I introduced three people to Ruth today

One said that without her I would be Ruthless

It seems that Ruth doesn't know that I'm alive
It seems that I don't know that she's not alive

Alive. . . Not Alive
What difference does it make?
All I know is that I love her

Even if she does wear the same outfit everyday.

Pick Up Poem

I'll be the sliced turkey and mayonnaise
      if you'll be the Wonder bread
I'll be the meatballs if you'll be the Hoagie Loaf
I'll be the stick shift if you'll change gears a lot
I'll be the high notes if you'll be the throat
I'll be many sheets of paper if you'll be the stapler
I'll be the telephone if you'll dial the numbers
I'll be the bullet if you'll be the Kennedy
I'll be the straw if you'll be the drink lid
I'll be the liquid if you'll be the goblet
I'll be disco if you'll be the seventies
I'll be the government if you'll be the revolution
I'll be the environment if you'll be recyclable
I'll be flapjacks if you'll be Aunt Jemimah
and I'll be the dirt if you'll be the hoe

What's your sign? Your place or mine?
Yeah, I'm into free love,
Oh, and equality too
Honey, your eyes are like the stars.

I'm The Writer

My girl,
She bakes.
Baklava.
I watch
Not that I can't help.
Oh, I can layer filo with the best of them.
You know, them, the people who layer filo dough.
Is it "f-eye-low" or "Fee-low"?
I don't know.
It tastes good though.
I like watching her layer filo.
I am a baklava voyeur.
She brushes butter on the layers.
She knows I am watching.
She is a butter brushing exhibitionist.
She's also beautiful.
You should see the way she puts on socks.
But that's not important to this poem.
I just thought I'd mention it.

My Girlfriend's Breasts

I bring my girlfriend's picture to work everyday
put it on my desk so I'm not lonely
My fellow employees stop by

>"Is that your girlfriend?"
>"Yes."
>"She's pretty."
>"Thank you."

The other day my girlfriend gave me her breasts
I took them into work
Put one on the desk next to her picture
My fellow employees stopped by

>"Is that your girlfriend's breast?"
>"Yes."
>"It's pretty."
>"Thank you."

The supervisor came by
Took the breast away
Said it was distracting from the work environment
She would give it back to me at the end of the day

>"That's okay" I thought to myself slyly
I still had the other breast in my backpack

No Girlfriend - No Stuff

Ex-girlfriend
She's got my books
She's got my video
She's got my Teddy Bear
Dumped me two years ago
Never did the post-relationship-stuff-exchange
She still has my stuff
And I've got nothing
No girlfriend
No stuff

Unexpected Lips

Your unexpected lips
that night in the rain
felt good against mine.
If I'd known they were coming
I'd have baked a cake

You

You are art incarnate
A living canvas with lungs and legs
Primary colors
mixed with natural tones
A landscape to behold
Three dimensional
Excellent use of perspective
I want to see you again
Make you part of my permanent collection
Allow occasional private showings
Maybe make a coffee table book
You are art incarnate
It's almost as if Monet brought you here
and left you on my couch

What She Does For Me

She sews the rips in my jacket
making it whole again
This is a metaphor
for everything she does for me

apartment life

Tupperware

I had a vision
in which every day
Once a day
I stood on the balcony of my apartment
and tossed a piece of Tupperware into the swimming pool.
I would do this early in the morning
before anyone was awake.

Every afternoon
The manager would fish the tupperware out of the pool
muttering obscenities under her breath.
"Damn Tupperware" she would say
"Where's it coming from?
Damn Tupperware!"

This would continue
until I ran out of Tupperware
and the manager would go insane
and drown in the pool.
Her lifeless body would float
with the Tupperware bobbing alongside.

The owner would hire a new manager
and I would buy some new Tupperware
and it would all start over.

That was my vision
And it was glorious.

Roommate's Head Sandwich Power Struggle

There I stood in the kitchen
A slice of wheat bread in each hand
My roommate innocently watching TV in the next room.
I ran in there
Stood in front of him
and firmly pressed each slice into his face.
I had made a Roommate's Head Sandwich
I glared at him and gritted my teeth
as if to convince him that I was about to eat his head off
and there would be nothing he could do about it.
He was confused.
This was a new experience for both of us.
I removed the bread from his face
took a bite out of one of the slices
and growled.
This was to show him my power in the situation.
Satisfied with my statement,
I calmly returned to the kitchen.
Later, he commented that the bread was cold against his
cheeks.
I told him that next time he might not be so lucky.

Archaeology

Two weeks of dust on my piano
another thousand years of this
and my apartment becomes an archeological dig.
The Romans would be in better shape today
if they kept up with the dusting.

Cactus Betrayal

My roommate confronted me with a cactus
he found in the kitchen.
I told him that I had never seen that cactus before
It must have been our other roommate's cactus
And he began to weep.
As if I had betrayed him with a cactus.

Apartment

I have two roommates
one is a Christian
one is a Muslim
and I am a Jew.
Our apartment is the old city,
Jerusalem.

Hanging in the Christian's room is a crucifix,
In the Muslim's room is a poster of people praying in Mecca,
and in my room, there is an Israeli flag,
and sometimes a giant gefilte fish.

Sometimes the Christian comes into my room
and accuses me of killing his messiah,
only in this case, it's Ella Fitzgerald.
Although everyone knows that Ella Fitzgerald died of old age,
her death remains a source of awkwardness between us.

Once I threatened to annex the Muslim's bedroom
unless he withdrew
the garbage from the kitchen.
He responded by blowing up my bathroom.
No-one was injured except for my cat
whose whiskers where a little singed.
I declared an apartment-wide day of remembrance
for my cat's heroic deeds.
Why not?
I have so many holidays,
What's one more?

Amidst all the turbulence,
we still manage to pay rent and share resources,
Water . . . food . . . cable.
We're catching up with the west
and our apartment exists as a paradigm for world peace.

geography

Why I like a living in Los Angeles
(because everyone always asks)

In Fairbanks, Alaska,
there is a law prohibiting Moose
from having sex in city streets.

In Ventura County, California,
it is illegal for dogs or cats to have sex
without a permit.

In Kingsville, Texas,
there is a law which prohibits two pigs
from having sex on airport property.

There are no such laws in Los Angeles.

I am proud and comforted to live
in a community where animals are free
to rampantly hump in public areas
without regulation.

This is why I like living in Los Angeles.

Five Dollar Sunglasses and Venice Pizza

Venice Beach
Walking along the boardwalk
Roller Skating Guitar Man sings for me.
I say "Didn't you open for Jane's Addiction once?"
He doesn't answer
Sings on.
When finished he says "You gotta buy one of my CD's man."
I tell him I only have enough for five dollar sunglasses
and a slice of Venice Pizza
He tells me I will amass wealth.
I tell him I will come back when I do.

I find the sunglasses booth
The one I always go to.
They have the sunglasses I want.
I pick them up and hand the man five dollars.
No words are exchanged
Just money and sunglasses
I knew they would be five dollars.
He knew enough not to ask for more.
I was obviously an experienced
Venice Beach Sunglasses buyer.

A trip to Venice is not complete without
a slice of Venice Pizza.
It's not good pizza.
It's not cheap pizza.
It's Venice Pizza, and it must be eaten
Or your trip to Venice is invalidated
As if it never happened.

I continue walking
New five dollar glasses on face
Slice of Venice Pizza in hand.
Man shouts at me

"Hey Pizza Boy! My Dick is harder than Superman's Elbow!"
I tell him that my butt cheeks are like Kryptonite.
He backs off
I have earned his respect.

I finish the pizza
Drive home
It is chilly on the boardwalk today.

Santa Monica Boulevard Halloween

the man
on Santa Monica Boulevard
who got out of his car
at the red light
wearing a dress
and a mask
who danced
and lifted up his skirt
so we could see his
underwear
and generous belly
jiggling
as he did a furious jig
for the entire duration of
the red light
while a van-load of women
to my left
who all had blonde hair
were smiling
and laughing
and waving
while a blue haired woman
sat in the passengers seat
of my car
contemplating becoming
the gothic homecoming queen
of Cleveland High School
until the light changed
and the masked cross dresser
got back in his car
and we all drove away
and the blonde women
later waved to me
on the freeway
this really happened
I'm not making it up

Saratoga I

I sit amongst the trees
Redwoods
Lots of them.

I look up.
The tops of the trees
and the sky
are the same place.
They are taller than anyone will ever be

I look down
hundreds of baby trees
the redwoods have been busy
the redwoods will outlive every one,
I hope.

I sit amongst the trees
it is quiet here
The trees don't tolerate any tomfoolery.

Saratoga II

Since I've arrived here
A bug has bitten me
another one moved into my eyelash
and another one burrowed into my arm.
I'm beginning to decompose
and will return to the Earth
much sooner than scheduled.

Burbank Airport (not Saratoga)

Flying into Burbank Airport
I realize that it is an ugly airport
Ugly like the brown viscous air you slice through
as you descend into the Valley
Ugly like the smell wafting out of the trash cans at gate A2
Ugly like the slimy ooze which coats your fingers
when you press them against the men's bathroom door when
exiting

There are beautiful airports in the world.
Airports like Pittsburgh
With its voice guided people walk,
Or Milwaukee with its well stocked used bookstore
Or San Jose
with its Parisian cafe
nestled in front of the Southwest Airlines gates.

In the men's bathroom in the San Jose airport
you don't have to touch anything.

The toilets, sinks and hand dryers
are all equipped with beams
that know whether or not you are there.
They flush, flow and blow automatically.
I recommend traveling to the San Jose International Airport
for the ultimate in airport bathroom experiences.

Yes. It is an international airport
It goes to Canada
Canada is a foreign country
Though most people in the United States are not aware of this.
I have been asked by the Canadians to point this out.
They would also like everyone

to send back all the Canadian pennies we've been collecting.
They plan on melting them down to make tanks
for their North American invasion force.
Their first target is North Dakota.
This is all secret information
So please don't tell anyone.

I am sitting in the Burbank Airport
contemplating Canadian invasion.
This is an ugly thought.
It compliments this ugly airport.

I am sitting in the Burbank airport
where
I have learned the way to San Jose.

Mission Viejo

Driving down the 101
to the 134
to the 210
to the 57
to the 5
to Mission Viejo
It is raining
I am listening to jazz the whole way
Be-bop
Straight ahead
the whole thing.
I am feeling very bohemian.
I arrive in Mission Viejo early
to avoid traffic.
So I go to the Mission Viejo Mall.
There I see
101 Dalmations.
My Bohemian fantasy comes to a crashing halt.
The dogs are cute,
but there's nothing artsy fartsy about them.
It gets worse.
I go into the Gap.
There I discover a 58 dollar flannel shirt.
I feel I am losing my artistic edge.
I am no longer prepared to go to a poetry reading.
Something needs to be done.
I walk out into the hallway of the mall.
(the mallway)
I scream at the top of my lungs
"COME AND SEE MY COLLECTION OF COCK RINGS!
VIVA LA BOHEME!"

I am quickly escorted to my car.
I feel much better.
I am ready for the reading.
It is important
to always live as an artist.

Menlo Park

I

In Menlo Park
there are legions of people
who help you pick out what to wear.
So that's one last thing to worry about.

II

I'm watching my friend put on deodorant
She says hello in her silly voice
as if to draw attention away
from the deodorant putting on.
It almost works.

III

I am once again surrounded by feminists
and continue to become more like them.
I just had a conversation with one
about hanging a dress over a portrait of George Washington.
It's beginning to make sense.

IV

They discuss discordant furniture wood instances in their house
which makes me think
they'd have a heart attack in mine,
the discordant everything museum.

food and drink

Vegetarian Poem

People who eat meat
should take a bite
out of a living cow
and then
spit in Flipper's eye

Pork Pizza

I called up Dominos on the phone
and they answered and said hello Dominos
and I said hello I'd like to order a pizza
and they said fine
that's what we do here
we make pizzas
and I said fine
I want pork on my pizza
and they said fine
how would you like your pork
and I paused
I thought
and I replied
I said
I want you to take a live pig
sprinkle some mozzarella cheese on it
and then set it free in my neighborhood
so I can hunt
I want to hunt for my pizza
and they said fine
that's the way we usually do it
you want a Pepsi with that?
and I said no
and they said fine
Twelve dollars.

Big Pasta

I walk into the kitchen
carrying pasta two feet long
Hey
says my roommate
be careful
you can poke an eye out with that.
I assure him that I am well aware
of the ramifications
of Big Pasta.

Identity Crisis

One day
I chopped my body up
into little pieces
because you are what you eat
and I was having an identity crisis.

Dirty Coffee

I hate drinking coffee in the morning
Because coffee is a dirty drink.
I hate getting dirty in the morning.
The night is for dirt.
I like being dirty at night.
Sitting in the dirty dark,
Surrounded by dirty people,
Thinking dirty thoughts,
Drinking dirty coffee.
I like being dirty at night.
In the morning,
I'd rather have an orange.

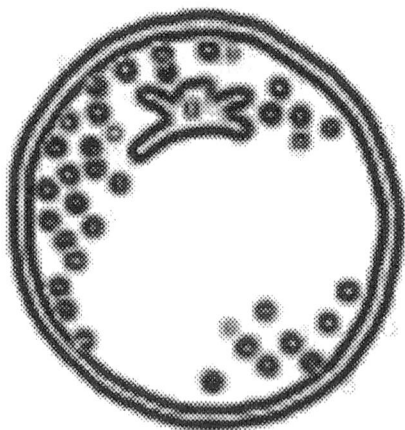

Coffee Is Not a Drink For Pussies

Coffee is not a drink for pussies
It's a serious beverage commitment
Dark
Dirty
Bad for your teeth
Bad for your brain

Coffee is not a drink for pussies
one drop
will stain your shirt
Forever

Coffee is not a drink for pussies
I'm sure it causes cancer
Leprosy
Male pattern baldness
Female pattern baldness
Premature ejaculation
Under-cooked omelettes

Coffee is not a drink for pussies
It is hot like the Equator
Bitter like four year old milk
Black like Nigeria
When you drink coffee
It's like you're drinking Nigeria

Coffee is not a drink for pussies
Don't talk to me about Lattes
Mother Fucker

Blender

That's one fuck of a blender
I comment as you stir-fry the tomatoes
solid metal base
one button
on and off.
It's such a fuck of a blender
you don't need multiple speeds.
You don't even need other appliances,
Stoves
electric can openers
Microwaves,
Not with that blender,
It's the blender for people
who take their blending very seriously.
The kind of blender your grandmother started to use
when she was 5.
That's one fuck of a blender

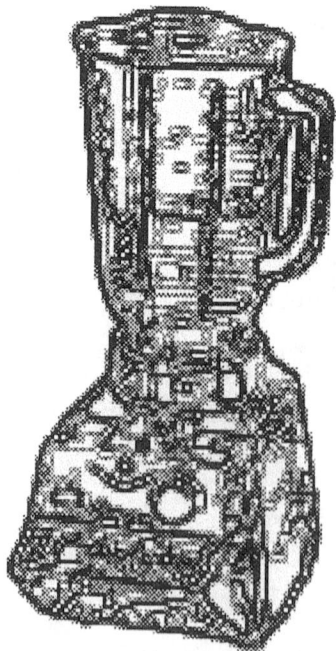

Appliance Drawing Girl

I knew a girl
who when she got bored
drew pictures of kitchen appliances
I caught her in mid-refrigerator once
I asked her to draw me a blender
I have a thing about blenders
She said *In a moment*
She hadn't drawn in the ice maker yet.

Jack and Leo on the Row

Jack and Leo on the Row
walking to nowhere
the street refugees
write poetry on the building walls
as skyscrapers are erected over them
The skyscrapers don't notice Jack and Leo
as they leave their cardboard condos
to stand in a street line
full of people
waiting for
a portion of spaghetti

Sandwich

I ordered a sandwich at the coffee shop
An hour went by and I still hadn't received it yet.
My stomach rumbled as if to remind me.
I asked the counter man about it and he assured me that
       he hadn't forgotten.
The bread was still in the oven,

Two days passed.

I was becoming quite hungry.
The counter man admitted that it might have slipped his mind.
"What had slipped his mind" I asked.
"The sandwich you ordered" he answered.
It had slipped my mind too.
We agreed that I should get the sandwich soon.
There was such a resolution to our agreement that we didn't
think about it again for a week.
By this time I was famished.

It was the stomach pains which caused me to say
       to the counter man

"Say, what about that sandwich."
He said "Oh yeah, your sandwich.
I'll put three of my best people on it."

And so he did,

and six days later,
the sandwich was delivered to my table.
Apparently it had been ready for a day and a half,
but some things had come up that they needed to take care of.
They apologized for the delay,
and gave me a free Diet-Coke for my patience.

By this time,
my body was so horribly emaciated,
that the Coke flowed down the new craters in my skin,
like Niagara Falls just met the Grand Canyon
at the screening of a new artsy film.

This was my Doug Knott Metaphor.

I requested that the sandwich be liquified,
and then fed to me intravenously.

Three weeks later,
they complied with this request.
But by this time
I had permanent brian damage,
scurvy,
and had lost the use of my legs and arms.

Needless to say this was reflected in their tip.

I dictated a letter to the management.
People were scolded,
New policies were developed.
It is good to be a consumer activist.

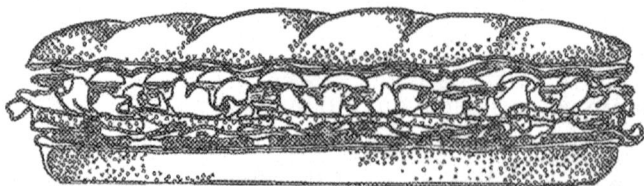

animals
(mostly insects)

Ants

Today at lunch I was God.
The hungry masses gathered around me.
I rained bread from their sky.
It was French bread
No Manna from this deity
I am a gourmet God
The crumbs of my lunch fed thousands
They were brought as offerings to their queen
They sculpted busts of me out of the larger pieces
They constructed temples in my honor out of hollowed out crusts
I was only there for a half hour
I won't return tomorrow
I may never
I will become part of their mythology
Holy wars will be fought in my name
Not that they know my name
They will call me food
And someday, they will eat me.

Ants and Gravity

Gravity means nothing to ants
I think
as I observe them walking up and down a tree
as if it was their interstate highway.
Things would be a lot different
if I could walk up and down trees.

No Fish Blues

I won a green rubber snake at a carnival
But it was an empty victory
As the snake was just a consolation prize
And thus a symbol
of my inability to win a goldfish

I Am Like My Cat

I am like my cat
perched
watching everything intently
with a third eye
Only I don't attack people
and try to eat their elbows.

It's Not Safe to Trip and Fly

I make red and blue strobe
like Superman on a Kryptonite trip
minus the yellow

flash flash flash
It's not safe to trip and fly

> Might drop the woman
> Might smash the planet
> Might forget to feed the dog

Super Dog barked his super barks
Buried his bones super deep and
Was paper trained so he wouldn't super shit on the rug

lick lick lick
Super Dog Super Saliva

Whoever thought up Super Dog
was on a Kryptonite trip

It's not safe to trip and fly

Doctor Frankenstein Caterpillar Killer

Frankenstein's monster was brought to life by electricity
This knowledge led me to my experiment with
the caterpillar and the 9 volt batteries
My pet caterpillar had drowned in his water dish
I thought I could revive him by placing his wet caterpillar
body between two nine volts
It didn't work the same
When frankenstein finished
He had a thinking, breathing, feeling monster.
When I finished,
I had two caterpillar halves.
Herbie.
That was the name of my pet caterpillar.
Was.
I buried him in the sandbox
No-one came to the funeral.

stories

The House of Small Things in Piedmont

The first thing that happened when I arrived at the house of small things in Piedmont was a discussion of whether or not I could play the ukulele. I said that I wasn't sure what a ukulele was and they told me it was like a small guitar. Later that evening I found the ukulele and it was, indeed, small.

As I sat figuring how to play it, I noticed on the other side of the room was a very small upright piano. The piano almost came up to my knee and was proportioned to a regular piano even smaller than the ukulele was to a guitar.

I began to suspect that this house might contain small versions of all musical instruments. But what happened next proved to me that I was in a house full of smaller versions of many kinds of objects.

On the small table next to me was the smallest French/English dictionary I had ever seen. It was so small that I could fit the entire thing into my mouth. I opened up the dictionary and co-incidentally the page I opened to was the one that had the word mouth on it.

So I did put the whole dictionary in my mouth to prove my theory that I could and to not test karma.

I walked around the house showing people what I had done. Everyone was pleased with my accomplishment. I was especially pleased that I had the entire French language on the tip of my tongue.

The house in Piedmont was on a hill overlooking the entire San Francisco Bay area. From the windows, San Francisco seemed to be very small. I knew that San Francisco was bigger than that. I figured it was just another effect of being in the House of small Things in Piedmont.

The Least Successful Man In The World

I know the story of the least successful man in the world. I'm going to tell you his story, so you'll know it too.

The least successful man in the world was born of Eskimos in northern Alaska where the temperatures can drop to seventy five degrees below zero in the summer. He saw that there was an abundance of snow and decided to capitalize on this by making his fortune selling snow cones to the people in his home town.

The name of his home town was Frozen Solid Watermelon. By remarkable coincidence this was also the of his sister.

The least successful man in the world made a crucial marketing error. He attempted to sell his snow cones in the dead of the coldest winter. He also didn't add any flavoring to the snow. He also neglected to buy cones to put the snow in. He would walk up to people in the freezing cold streets of Frozen Solid Watermelon, pick up a handful of snow, and try to sell it as a snow cone.

He didn't sell a single one of his snow cones. This made him very sad. So sad, that he would stand in the streets clutching snow, at the end of a long day of not selling snow cones and cry desperately out loud

"Why doesn't anybody want to buy any snow cones? Icy cold, fresh from snow, snow cones. Doesn't anybody want to buy a snow cone?"

After several months of this his sister, Frozen Solid Watermelon, confronted him and said

"You idiot. Why don't you sell something hot? Nobody wants to buy snow cones here. IT'S TOO COLD!"

He was very embarrassed and devastated by his sister's words. But he saw the wisdom in them. He developed a new strategy for success. He decided that he would sell hot cocoa and become a rich man doing so. But he was too embarrassed to remain in Frozen Solid Watermelon because of his recent snow cone-related fiasco. So he packed all of his belongings and moved as far away as he could.

He ended up in a medium sized village located eight miles north of the equator. The name of the village was Burst Into Flames Anus. Coincidentally, this was also the of his travel agent.

In the village of Burst Into Flames Anus the temperature never dropped below one hundred and thirty degrees. Although one week in August is so hot, that it actually seems cold. During this week, all the residents of Burst Into Flames Anus put on sweaters and wool underwear and sit around at home singing songs about Hawaii and apartment renovation.

The least successful man in the world arrived in the village in December. He stole a cart from a local supermarket, gathered aluminum cans from alleys and landfills, put sea water in each one of them, mixed in some hot cocoa mix, and set the whole cart on fire, until the cans glowed red, and the liquid inside boiled out the top.

He doused the flaming cart with a fire extinguisher he had borrowed from an apartment building, setting off the alarm, which caused the two hundred thirteen residents to immediately vacate, most of whom leapt to their deaths out of their apartment windows.

The least successful man in the world walked up and down the streets of Burst Into Flames Anus with his cart shouting

"Hot cocoa here! Piping hot cocoa! It'll warm you right up!"

On this particular day it was one hundred and sixty eight degrees outside. No one wanted to buy his hot cocoa and he received several third degree burns holding up the cans to show them to people.

At the end of a week, he sat on a curb weeping. He had spent all of his money on the cocoa mix. He had no more matches to keep his product warm. He was devastated. He cried out loud "Why doesn't anybody want to buy my hot cocoa?!"
As fate would have it, the least successful man in the world

happened to be sitting on the curb in front of the Burst Into Flames Anus Police Station. The police force of Burst Into Flames Anus were a patriotic bunch. They loved their country more than they loved their wives; but not quite as much as they loved beer. They were also a very unsympathetic group of people.

When they overheard the least successful man in the world say

"Why doesn't anybody want to buy my hot cocoa?!"

They were enraged. It just so happened that in their native language, this was the most insulting thing that anyone could say. It would be impossible to give an exact translation; but it was similar to saying

"Living in this country is worse than rubbing donkey shit all over your body, and then rubbing camel shit all over the donkey shit, and then washing it off, and then rubbing more camel shit on you, but concentrating more on the face this time, and then having an asexual baboon spit coconut rind on your mother's face."

And so the police force of Burst Into Flames Anus were so incensed by his misfortunate comment that they came outside, and took turns bludgeoning him to death. After he was dead sixteen times, they went back into the station and resumed their beer drinking.

And so the least Successful man in the world lay dead in the streets of Burst Into Flames Anus. His travel agent, Burst Into Flames Anus, came to identify the body, and then packaged the remains and put them in the mail back to Frozen Solid Watermelon.

Unfortunately the remains never arrived, because they accidentally fell out of the plane and landed in the Bermuda Triangle. There they were eaten by the Lochness Monster and Bigfoot, both of whom happened to be vacationing there at the time. The Bermuda Triangle is where all of those kinds of people go to vacation.

This has been the story of the least successful man in the world.

giant hoochie dinosaurs that lick your eyeballs

The Lone Mosher

The Lone Mosher
No-one to bump into
Moves around
alone

The Lone Mosher
venting his frustrations
beats himself up

The Lone mosher
is bleeding
self inflicted mosh wounds
Someone should get him some blow up mosher dolls
        to mosh with

The Lone Mosher
Proves his manliness
to himself

Untitled

This poem is called
Jesus had a penis and all Christians are maniacs
This poem is called
Moses had a penis and all Jews are maniacs
This poem is called
Mohammed had a penis and all Moslems are maniacs
This poem is called
Buddha had a penis but his tummy was sexier
This poem is called
Confucius had a penis Confucius say
This poem is called
I am sodomized by Satan every single night
This poem is called
all pagan witches have penises and they brew them up
in a cauldron to make pagan witch penis stew
This poem is called
Darwin was right and I saw his penis in a museum
This poem is called
Richard Nixon had a penis and so did Checkers
This poem is untitled
because there are far too many penises in the world

The Poet

The Poet
got up to read
took off all his clothes
read naked.
I could tell right away he wasn't Jewish.

Serious Poetry Format (for AS)

All the people who are stupid
With their stupid ideas
and all the other bad things in the world
So I made them drink my urine
Except that guy
Cuz he has an afro
and afros are cool.
Add final cynical judgement.
BOYEE!

Creamsicle (for Brendan Constantine)

I arrived at the event early,
you were just walking out to your car.
I greeted you by singing "Take the skinheads bowling, take
them bowling."
You looked up and then said to me:
"I'm going to get cream,
you can't have a fucking reading without cream for the coffee."
and then you got in your car and drove away.
I was disappointed
because I wanted to say funny things to you,
and listen to the funny things that you had to say.
Later, after the reading, we finally got to talk.
I told you that I should have just gotten in the car
and gone to get cream with you.
you said
"No...it was awful, I had to go to two stores before I found one
that even had cream."
I appreciated your attempt to shield me from
the unpleasantness of your cream getting experience.
But imagine this.
You and me
in the car
together
going to get cream
together . . .
We would have been above the law.
We would have been the two musketeers,
the two amigos,
the two caballeros,
peanut butter and jelly,
cinnamon and toast,
syrup and bubbles,
Rogaine and bald people,
Paris and cheese,
naked people and burned down clothing stores.
We would have been a party,
a fiesta,
a ho-down,
a bar mitzvah with an attitude,
and the world would have been our fucking creamsicle.

Titles of Pieces That Didn't Make It Into This Book

Walt Disney, Man or Sadistic Buffalo Confuser

The Sexual Implications of the Wizard of Oz

A festival of Rubber Chickens

I Hate Decorative Soaps

Dating Advice From a Nine Year Old Stud

The Bastards Stole My Cheese

Snakes and Humanity

The Fleeting Fame of Pogs

Foot Health Month

Bikini's Demand Justice

epilogue

I Am My Own Orange County

Walking down the street one evening
I came across a man
sitting at a table
outside of a Mexican Restaurant
Smoking a cigarette
Wearing a beret
and playing cards.

I stopped walking
Looked at the guy
In the eye
and said to him

"You're a Mexican food eating
cigarette smoking
beret wearing
card playing
mother fucker."

The man stood up
and punched out my eye.
Fortunately I had another eye
and I walked away
having stowed my knocked out eye
in my jacket pocket.

Walking down the street one evening

(I can't tell you how many poems I've began with "walking
down the street", or "driving down the street", or "sitting in
the coffee house." It's either a personal trademark or proof of
my inadequacy as a supposed creative individual.)

I came across a man

(A man, a woman, a child, a dog, a shopping card, it's always something. Get to the point Lupert.)

sitting at a table
outside of a Mexican Restaurant
Smoking a cigarette
Wearing a beret
and playing cards.

(Holy crap-crap! This is typical of my inclusion of ultra-mun-
dane details in an effort to imply that their ensemble creates
something spectacular. I'm not even buying it anymore.)

I stopped walking
Looked at the guy
In the eye

(Three phrases of a sentence included to build suspense. Oooh,
I'm on the edge of my seat. Will this tension ever cease? Lay
down your hat Stephen King, the Supreme Suspender has ar-
rived!)

and said to him

"You're a Mexican food eating
cigarette smoking
beret wearing
card playing
mother fucker."

(As if saying these words is anything more than translucent
evidence that nothing at all interesting was going to happen,
so I had to make up farcical stories of cussing out a random
person in such a way that no-one could possibly believe that it
ever happened and causing most people to stop reading or lis-
tening at exactly this point.)

The man stood up

(This is the climax of the piece, which is sad because no-one is ready to climax, no-one has even considered climaxing, and as a result of what has been written so far, at least a dozen people have contemplated giving up climaxing altogether.)

and punched out my eye.

(Typical of my last ditch efforts to utilize the absurd and imply that everything should be re-read with a third eye as if some elements of genius were woven in-between the text so far. It's time I increased my medication. Also, the phrase has an almost Hal Sirowitzian diction about it which is brilliant when delivered by Hal Sirowitz and invariably lost when I attempt it.)

Fortunately I had another eye

(Another attempt at furthering the absurd [see previous comments] only this one is even weaker than the first.)

and I walked away
having stowed my knocked out eye
in my jacket pocket.

(And so the poem ends, as if this was an ending, as if there was a tangible beginning, as if anything interesting happened in the middle. Because it wasn't, and it didn't, and it didn't, and no-one has gained any insights about anything, and we've wasted too much time, and the children in Africa are still starving.)

I'm glad I decided to walk tonight.

(And the critique has gone on for so long that additional lines had to be added to the poem.)

And suddenly the separation

(between poem and critique)

Becomes less coherent
(like)

We're all intoxicated.
We are all too
SELF CRITICAL
(genius)

Sheer genius.

Walking down the street one evening
I came across a man
sitting at a table
outside of a Mexican Restaurant
smoking a cigarette
wearing a beret
and playing cards.

I stopped walking
Looked at the guy
In the eye
and said to him

"You're a Mexican food eating
cigarette smoking
beret wearing
card playing
mother fucker."

The man stood up
and punched out my eye.
Fortunately I had another eye
and I walked away
having stowed my knocked out eye
in my jacket pocket.

I'm glad I decided to walk tonight.
Genius,
Sheer genius.

bonus material

(additional poems from the
I Am My Own Orange County "era")

Mister T

What in the world has happened to Mister T?
Mohawk gold-chained angry man
American Culture was good when Mister T. was at its forefront.

I want Mister T. back
I want him to come to my house
And I want him to bring Missus T.
Mister Junior T.
And Mister Baby T.

We'll have a party
We'll have a T Party
We'll have a Mr. T. Party.

I'll serve Mister Iced T.
and I'll mix it with Mister T's Bloody Mary Mix
When drinking we'll be referred to as Mister T. Totallers

When we get bored we'll play a rompingous game of Mister T. Ball.
And when our children grow up they'll be Mister T-nagers.

NASA will no longer say T-minus ten seconds and counting.
They will say Mister T-minus ten seconds and counting
They will will like it so much that they will add ten more seconds.
We'll watch it all on our Mister T-V's.

When Mister T. arrives again
Everyone will have mohawks
Everyone will have gold chains
Everyone will be outrageously angry
And Everyone will be black
Oh Mister T. Mister T.
Come back Mister T.
You are Americana
You are Africana Americana
Your are the only important cultural icon
We need you
We need you
We Mister T-eed you.

Come back Mister T.
Mister T.

Pick Up Poem (alternate version)

Say baby,
you wanna do something?
like what?
Well...

I'll be the sliced turkey and mayonnaise if you'll be the Hoagie
loaf
I'll be many sheets of paper if you'll be the stapler
I'll be disco if you'll be the seventies
I'll be a big gob of greasy hair if you'll be Pert Plus
I'll be unshaved stubble if you'll scrape yourself across my face
I'll be unsightly yellow plaque if you'll be Aquafreshy goodness
I'll be Sperm whales if you'll be the Pacific Ocean
I'll be flapjacks if you'll be Aunt Jemimah
I'll be the lava lamp if you'll be all oozy
I'll be the noise if you'll be the ear so I can just go in there
                and you'll all hear me.
I'll be the bullet if you'll be the Kennedy
I'll be the poisonous berries if you'll be the bush
I'll be the guy with guy genitals if you'll be the girl
                with girl genitals
and I'll be the dirt if you'll be the hoe.

What's your sign? Your place or mine?
Yeah, I'm into free love,
Oh, and equality too
Honey, your eyes are like the stars.

She Grabbed It

Standing up
watching a show
girl runs up behind me
grabs my ass
like it's a hundred dollar bill

She smiles at me like a wicked thief
I say "Hey"
but she's already making her getaway

Later
I see my ass at a hock shop on Van Nuys Boulevard
Forty Dollars
They could do better

She Was Many Things

She was a looker
    Eyes like outer space
    Lips like a Lamborghini
    Legs until Thursday

She had it going on
    Moved like a leopard
    Smelled like North Dakota
    Spoke like every movie made in nineteen fifty-three

She knew what was up
    Could see guys coming months in advance
    Predicted photosynthesis before it got big
    Could alphabetize humanity

She had certain skills
    Painted a pit bull yellow before it batted an eye
    Played instruments that hadn't been invented yet
    Drove a back-hoe with her teeth

She had some money
    Owned a fur-lined driveway
    Sent her furniture on a European vacation
    Paid for Algeria in cash

She was
    Electric
    Powered Brazil for a week with her ass

    Magnetic
    Sheets of metal flew at her when she walked down the street

    Eclectic
    Never said the same word twice . . . ever

She was some kind of lady
    my kind of woman

She was
    She was a looker

Shower in the Sink

Today I took a shower in the sink
It's not that I'm that short
There just wasn't a shower

Had to do it in shifts
My arms soaped up
while my legs read a magazine

Got to my ass
and my chest
was making a phone call

Rinsed shampoo out of my hair
while my ears discussed Rilke
with the towel rack

I am clean now
except for my thighs who
would have nothing to with the whole thing

I wish they were a little more open
but then again, I think that
about a lot of people's thighs

The Great Sugar Debacle

This is the story of the great Sugar Debacle
One night I was in my car with a beautiful woman
We were driving
We made the collective decision to go back to my house
and make cookies.
Once we had made this decision, I said
    "I may not have enough brown sugar for the cookies, so
let's go to the store."
She wasn't sure that I needed brown sugar for the cookies and
she said
    "I'm not sure that you need brown sugar for the cookies."
and I said
    "Oh yes, you need brown sugar for the cookies."
and she took my word for it and so we drove to the store
We walked into the store
We walked directly to the sugar aisle
I am so familiar with the store that I can walk directly
    to the sugar aisle
without so much as passing by the Cheerios or bananas.
And there was the brown sugar.
I quickly picked up a box of brown sugar.
She was inspired by this and said
    "I'm going to get some regular sugar for my home."
and I said
    "Great"
and so she picked a small box of white sugar
and we walked to the check out aisle.
There we put our sugars down next to each other
White and brown
like Thomas Jefferson and Sally Hemings.
If they were sugars.
I said to the checkout person
    "We have all our sugar bases covered."
The checkout person responded with something
so uninteresting that I don't even remember what it was.

My friend, the sugar buyer, paid for both boxes of sugar
She introduced this idea by saying
        "I'll pay for the sugar."
This was fine because earlier I had paid for the beverages.
I say 'beverages' as if I had mentioned them already
and I know that I haven't
but trust me
there were beverages.

We drove back to my apartment with the sugars
and this is where the Great Sugar Debacle happened.

We discovered that I already had a box of brown sugar
        in the cabinet.
That was part one of the great sugar debacle.

We made the cookies
We ate some of the cookies

Then she went home.
That was the second part of the great sugar debacle.

Back in my kitchen, I discovered
She had left her box of white sugar
Went home without it.

This was the third and final insult of the great sugar debacle.
Thank you for listening.

T-Hair

I want there to be a hair shop
where you could get a mohawk
because all they do is mohawks
even if you say "Just a little off the top and clean up the ends"
They wouldn't listen to you
and you'd walk out of there with a mohawk
and you couldn't do a thing about it
because the shop is called "Mohawk Hair Shop"
and you've signed a disclaimer
that gives them the legal right to make a mohawk out of your hair
And there's a sign on the wall that clearly states

     "ALL WE DO IS MOHAWKS"

and there's really fine print that says
"except on Thursdays when we do reverse mohawks
and charge double."

53 Guts

Realizing I had no guts I went down to the guts store
        to buy me some.
I figured I better get me some guts lickety split.
So I spoke with the sales associate at the guts store
And she asked me what kind of guts I wanted
And I asked her what kind of guts did they have
And she said they had all kinds of guts
but they specialized in gizzards.
I told her that I would take 53 gizzards,
And she wrapped 'em up
And I used my Visa
And now I've got guts.
53 Guts.

Self Polarization

Breasts attract me
like round magnets to my steel head
They polarize me
Make me want to stick
I am like Woolly Willy, Magnetic Dust Face Man
My Beard rearranges in their presence

Some Common Themes in My Poetry
or, a Future Table of Contents

Mr. T.
Goldfish
Naked
Girlfriend
No Girlfriend
Will you be my girlfriend?
I wish she was my girlfriend
The plight of the negro and others oppressed
The Moon

Naked Mr. T.
Naked goldfish
Naked girlfriends
Will you be my naked girlfriend
Will you be my naked oppressed negro
Let's get naked and become negroes and fly to the moon.

Let us worship Mr. T.
But only if he's naked
and only if he brings along his girlfriend
and we establish a naked colony
on the moon.

Liberate the naked goldfish
by disguising them as Mr. T.
and other famous negroes
and hiding them in a secret underground hideaway
on the moon.

Let's all get Mohawks and eat Sushi.

Condoms, Cigarettes and Vomiting

Condoms are expensive
but maybe you can split the cost with your sexual partner
Cigarettes are expensive
but maybe you could split the cost with your lungs
But that would be silly
as neither of your lungs have jobs, or vocational training
Maybe you could send your lungs to college
so they could get good jobs
And help to pay for those cigarettes
But that would take too much time
and you can't even afford to send yourself to college
So maybe your lungs could get jobs as waiters or waitresses
But that wouldn't work
because no one wants to be served a slice of quiche
        by a disembodied lung,
especially one as charred and black as yours
So maybe you'll have to pay for your cigarettes by yourself
Or maybe you should just quit smoking
as it's the most disgusting thing you can do
Besides perhaps vomiting in public
Though when you think about it,
you realize that smoking can KILL you
Whereas vomiting is cleansing
Then your sexual partner breaks up with you
So you have to pay for your condoms too
Then you go broke and bankrupt
Yes BOTH broke AND bankrupt
Having to buy condoms and cigarettes all the time
And soon you can't even afford those
So you sit around all day
And you spend most of your time vomiting.

Crossing The Street Is Dangerous

Crossing the street is dangerous
in your car, on your feet
Crossing the street is dangerous
earthquakes, drive by shootings
Crossing the street is dangerous
debris falling from outer space, smog
Crossing the street is dangerous
spontaneous human combustion, heart failure
Crossing the street is dangerous
wild animals escaped from the zoo, nazis
Crossing the street is dangerous
I just got run over by an ambulance

Epic Penis Poem

Let me tell you about my penis.
My penis is an exclusive secret agent of love.
My penis is on the guest list of clubs that I can't get into.
My penis arrives for dinner in a limousine provided by NBC,
while I show up fifteen minutes later in a jalopy.
My penis was invited to be the spokesperson for the
Coca-Cola Corporation.
My penis takes forty-five minute showers by itself.
My penis appeared in several major motion pictures and is
currently bidding for the lead role in the new Oliver Stone film
expose of the Reagan administration.
My penis speaks nine different languages and once negotiated a non-
aggression pact between Ethiopia and a country right next to Ethiopia.
My penis can fly an airplane and if asked will explain what went
wrong with the ValuJet flight in incredible technical detail.
My penis comes equipped with several pop open compartments
in which it stores a life raft, coffee maker, World Almanac and
Book of Facts, hair care products, several bars of gold bullion,
and breath freshener.
My penis once conducted The William Tell Overture, Beethoven's
Fifth Symphony, Also Sprach Zarathustra, and the theme to Star Wars.
Once, while I was away on a business trip, my penis re-arranged
all my furniture, alphabetized my compact discs, and ate my
roommates left leg.
My penis disguised itself as Santa Claus and got a job working
in a mall during the holidays.
My penis was invited to the White House for Dinner. I got to go too.
It said right on the invitation "Penis and Guest."
My penis has been used as currency in developing nations.
Sometimes my penis wears sunglasses to lay low and avoid
the paparazzi.
My penis spent a year dead for tax purposes.
There will be a test on my penis at the end of the week.
This has been the life story of my penis.

Hair Cutting Ass

Sitting in the chair
getting my hair cut
I notice the ass of the haircutter at the chair next to me
I look to my hair cutter as if to ask
How can you stand here and cut hair
with an ass like that standing next to you all day?
I wouldn't be able to do it.
I would be sculpting that ass into my customers' hair-dos.
That's one hell of a haircutting ass.

Beeper

I got a beeper and I put it on vibrate mode
and I strapped it to my penis
and I don't need women anymore
But I do need you to give me a call
because I am permanently attached
to the information super vibrating highway

My Shoe and Your Breast

Yeah, my shoe touched your breast
And you wrote a poem about it detailing the event to the world
But honey,
what you don't know
is that my shoe lives in its own separate breast touching reality
It often does things that I am not aware of
Once I got a call from Victoria's Secret
telling me my shoe was there
It had been trying on lace panties
It is a nasty shoe
and I am trapped with it
as since the earthquake
after much driving and looking and driving and looking
I have determined
that there are far too few shoe stores left in the valley

Bikini's Demand Justice

Standing on the bus saying goodbye to people
Person after person
Hug after Hug
I feel like I am in a receiving line
Someone says I would make a good Miss America
I say I don't think my breasts are right
They wouldn't do justice to a bikini in the swimsuit competition
and bikinis DEMAND justice

When it Rains

Two women in two days
It's my kind of weekend
And beautifully speaking
Tomorrow is only Sunday.

Hooters

Driving along I see a woman walking
with HOOTERS so big
They could carry her into outer space
They could float the Queen Mary
They could feed Africa
As they were hooters, they made me want to hoot
I went HOOT HOOT HOOT Hooters
But they didn't hear me
and neither did she
It was all for the better
as I was in my car with the window up and the music loud
and she was on the sidewalk with outside noise

What Goes Up

Blow job Friday
Locked door Sunday
Life has its ups and downs

Naked Drive

I felt so good about leaving work today
I took off my tie for the drive home

I felt so good about leaving work today
I unbuttoned my top button for the drive home

I felt so good about leaving work today
I took off my pants for the drive home

It went on like this and pretty soon I was naked
driving home

At first people driving along were shocked at the sight of me
But I showed them my removed tie
and gave them a thumbs up and a smile and
they began to understand

Pretty soon everyone on the freeway was driving home naked
It was a glorious day
They felt good
You could tell
Just by looking at them

Bus Driver Bitch

Bus Driver Bitch
Lost luggage
won't open the boot
Luggage not in there she says
"Please Bus Driver Bitch
Open the boot
Surely the lost luggage is there."
"I see no reason" she says
"I packed it myself
no lost luggage there."
"What would be the harm in checking?
We are three hours early
due to your racing light and sound
Not to mention risking our lives to get here."
"It will accomplish nothing." she says
I get angry.
I yell at her.
"You NEED to open the boot now
You work for me
You Bus Driver Bitch
Open that boot NOW
As if I have nothing to do but yell at bus drivers.
I have never yelled at a bus driver in my life
and I've known many!"
She weakens
Though inflamed.
She opens the boot
SO time consuming.
We may only be two hours early to our next stop.

Only two hours?
SATAN!

In the boot,
The lost luggage.

Bus Driver Bitch
Bus Driver Bitch

What were you going to do?
Take it home?
Try it on?
Ninth grade boys underwear?

Not today Bus Driver Bitch,
That's OUR LUGGAGE!

The Hitchhiking Palm Tree That I Didn't Stop To Pick Up

On the way home from work I saw a palm tree hitchhiking.
I almost stopped to pick it up
But I decided not to.
I never pick up hitchhikers
and I don't know what that palm tree would think
it's so goddamned special

Speed Bump Employment

One day I noticed that a particular speed bump
on a particular road
was not there.
Where did it go?
It had been there for years.
I guess it got a job on another road.
The new road probably pays better.

Watermelon Ode

Ah watermelon,
I eat you
Perfect food
Gift from God.
How excited I was to see you here
When all I expected
was a drink of mediocre iced tea.

Vending Machine Blues

The woman
frustrated
Pressed the wrong number
Sunchips instead of pretzels,
Explains her troubles to me
Bad eyes
Couldn't see the numbers
Thus sunchips
Sorrow,
As if she expects pretzels to fly out of my butt.

Moustache Civilization

There was once a majestic moustache mosaic
on the inside door of my living room closet.
There were many moustaches there,
all living harmoniously.

But one by one
The moustaches went away
I don't know where.
Leaving only one
A Big One
A GREAT BIG MOUSTACHE
It's bigger than all of the other moustaches were combined

I think it scared all the littler moustaches away.
I'm going to have to have a talk with that
        GREAT BIG MOUSTACHE
A talk about tolerance,
Especially tolerance of littler moustaches.

K-Mart Excitement

When I was very young
my mother would take me grocery shopping.
While she was picking out food,
I would go to the K-Mart next store.
Of course to the toy department.

Once,
I came across the Nerf football section.
I picked one up
Looked up and down the aisle,
No one was in sight

I hurled the football with all of my might
over the aisles
Across the store.
Thought it was a long time ago,
I seem to remember that it was in the direction
of the automotive or gardening departments.

I hard a crash and a scream in the distance.
K-Marts are big places.

I immediately left the store,
Returned to my mother
She had bought me a bunch of bananas as a surprise.
I was exhilarated,
But only partially because of the bananas.

Tuxedo Man

Enter Tuexedo man
Into the room.
Tuxedo man doesn't belong
Not while he's wearing that tuxedo.
Overdressed Tuxedo Man
No relation to Encinoman
Or Superman
Though they all have the same last name.

About The Author

The author at sea. (Sea not pictured)

Rick Lupert has been involved in the Los Angeles poetry community since 1990. He served for two years as a co-director of the Valley Contemporary Poets, a twenty-three year old non-profit organization which produces a regular reading series and publications out of the San Fernando Valley. His poetry has appeared in numerous magazines and literary journals, including *The Los Angeles Times*, *Chiron Review*, *Zuzu's Petals*, *Caffeine Magazine*, *Blue Satellite* and others. He recently edited *A Poet's Haggadah: Passover through the Eyes of Poets* anthology and is the author of ten other books: *Paris: It's The Cheese, Mowing Fargo, I'm a Jew. Are You?, Feeding Holy Cats, Stolen Mummies, I'd Like to Bake Your Goods, A Man With No Teeth Serves Us Breakfast* (Ain't Got No Press), *Lizard King of the Laundromat, Brendan Constantine is My Kind of Town* (Inevitable Press) and *Up Liberty's Skirt* (Cassowary Press). He has hosted the long running Cobalt Café reading series in Canoga Park since 1994 and is regularly featured at venues throughout Southern California.

Rick created and maintains the Poetry Super Highway, a major internet resource for poets. (PoetrySuperHighway.com)

Currently Rick works as the music teacher and graphic and web designer for Temple Ahavat Shalom in Northridge, CA and for anyone who would like to help pay his mortgage.

Rick's Other Books

A Man With No Teeth
Serves Us Breakfast
Ain't Got No Press
May, 2007

I'd Like to Bake Your Goods
Ain't Got No Press
January, 2006

STOLEN MUMMIES
Ain't Got No Press
February, 2003

BRENDAN CONSTANTINE IS
MY KIND OF TOWN
Inevitable Press
September, 2001

up liberty's skirt
Cassowary Press
March, 2001

FEEDING HOLY CATS
Cassowary Press
May, 2000

I'm a Jew, Are You?
Cassowary Press
May, 2000

MOWING FARGO
Sacred Beverage Press
December, 1998

Lizard King of the Laundromat
The Inevitable Press
February, 1998

Paris: It's The Cheese
Ain't Got No Press
May, 1996

For more information:
http://PoetrySuperHighway.com/

www.ingramcontent.com/pod-product-compliance
Lightning Source LLC
Chambersburg PA
CBHW061957040426
42447CB00010B/1793